In the House Magisterial

poems by

Seth Jani

Finishing Line Press
Georgetown, Kentucky

In the House Magisterial

ACKNOWLEDGMENTS

The author wishes to gratefully acknowledge the journals in which many of
these poems first appeared:

Abyss & Apex: "Images"
The Blue Hour: "In the House Magisterial," "Old Honey," "Wild Pears"
Dămfino: "Beach Relic"
ExFic: "Signals for Belief"
Foliate Oak: "Meditation on a Sunporch in Maine"
Grasslimb: "Some Goals for the Year"
The Hamilton Stone Review: "Lantern"
Hawai`i Pacific Review: "Trees from Eight Angles"
Milk Sugar: "Clockwork," "From the Window at 2 AM"
Peacock Journal: "Letting It Be"
Random Sample: "Incantation"
Semaphore Magazine: "Creatures"
Sentinel Literary Quarterly: "Alembic"
Subliminal Interiors: "Landscape in November"
Verse-Virtual: "Force," "Porthole"

Publisher: Leah Maines
Editor: Christen Kincaid
Cover Art: "Garden of Time" by Dimitris K.
        Istock.com/dimitris_k
Author Photo: Taryn Hendrix
Cover Design: Elizabeth Maines McCleavy

Printed in the USA on acid-free paper.
Order online: www.finishinglinepress.com
        also available on amazon.com

Author inquiries and mail orders:
Finishing Line Press
P. O. Box 1626
Georgetown, Kentucky 40324
U. S. A.

Table of Contents

Some Goals for the Year

To make the night work.
To make the darkness reluctantly fearful.
To make the body sturdy as a switch
In evil weather.
To make the dream pivot and jive.
And certainly to make the old, half-starved
Warhorse of the heart
Lay down in the blaze of autumn,
Ears perked to heaven,
Happy for some hay.

Off the Map

The heart is a liminal country
Outside the cartographer's eye.
Its streams are glimmering and indistinct.
Its inhabitants, mysterious and starved.
The altars there are offered up
To the inexpressibly boundless,
Obsessed with night stars and forges underfoot,
Entirely removed from the mind's
Sun-bound focus,
The reliable dimensions of daylight.

Its boundaries shift and shine
With the moon's partial darkness.

Its waters race down, strange and measureless
As the latitudes of sleep.

Landscape in November

The mansion in the ochre light
That only appears, late fall,
At the edge of the frost's dominion.
You make a pilgrimage through
The eddying leaves
Certain there is a door
In the twisted arch of treetops.
November is nature's preferred thoroughfare
Between the living and the dead,
The wet musical season bridging arrivals.
You climb the skeletal branches,
Poke your head among the bone-white birch limbs,
Await the element that is not quite snow
And not quite rain.
You lay down upon the cool, moistened earth
Wrapped between your past and future life,
Blinking the mysterious present
In and out of being.

Coming Home

Like the lanterns in the mind
We urge to never go out,
The sun travels backwards
Down beyond the edge
Where our own horizons do not reach,
And we are left with the cool autumn dark
Touching our bodies, as clear and tenuous as glass.
We too have made our pact
With some other horizon in the night,
Have promised an inexplicable vista
That we would return,
Would come back trailing
Our cloudy kerchiefs in the wind,
Would come back like devotees
Returning to their families and trades
After a year of pilgrimage.
And so on these nights which speak
Mysteriously of harvest and death
It is like a reunion with some memory
Inscribed inside our bodies,
A rhythm etched into our bone.
It is like coming home
In the middle of savage snowdrifts
To light a tiny candle in your room,
Because you're sure some far-off friend
Was meant to find you
But can't decide what's needed more:
The light to guide them through the forest,
Or the friend to hold you in the dark.

Letting It Be

I would walk down this street forever,
With the rain hitched to my side
(old elemental companion of my youth)
And the early moon flowering above the city,
Above the lonely light of coffee shops,
Above the disenchanted, unemployed smokers
Howling from rooftops, or flaring up
In the dark of alleys.
I would walk this street
As though I were coming home
To the one clear spot inside myself,
The only safety I have known.
I would walk this street
And let the singular earth,
With its habit of letting sadness exist,
Continue on, beneath the soaking plastic
Of my shoes.
I would let it be alive, with all its
Broken happenstance, inside my body.
And if nothing but a single bird
Ever crossed my path,
The most ordinary swallow or jay,
I would let it remain, joyful and undisturbed,
In the middle of whatever troubled road
I happened to be on.

Porthole

Those hours spent infinitely alone
In the gray washes of morning light.

The childhood hand reaching through
A pause in the curvature of time

To grasp an apple eaten long ago,
A kiss forgotten by the mouth.

The plot of a life halfway lived
Is backed by the ghosts of memory.

What is still unborn moves
Towards us,

A single, radial star
In the blizzard's canvas.

Incantation

I want to enter fully into midnight,
The bookish dark of winter,
The unhewn plentitude
Poked through with stars
And treetops.

I want to carry the singing
Into my own unlit body,
The primitive anthem of
Birds at dusk,
The cricket's carol of sundown,

Each moving through my blood
Homebound on its reddened current.
I want to believe that I can embrace
As fruitfully as sunlight
The strange interior of earth,

Can find my own black portal
And lay down with that bruised
Underworldly music.
An orphic ear cocked to listen.
A shuddering heart native to the dark.

Clockwork

Spring night and the world
Moving towards forgetfulness.
The liminal music of wind and trees
Pigeon-holed by someone's talentless playing.
We go stumbling from one end of life to another
Breeding the captive inside us.

Whatever is divine, borders on drunkenness.

Whatever is petty, erratically flickers.

In the sure-fire light of desire
We push the body towards some
Secret fate.
Believing not in decay, but in angels.
The small imaginal truth that we are born
To rise-up
Utterly transfigured.

The unprovable certainty that whatever
Revolutions make the cosmos tick,
Also make our own hearts tinker and dream.

Beach Relic

Then I was alone with the ghost,
With the daylit ocean coming towards me,
The mercurial water with parted lips
Not still, but singing.

From each end of the darkened shoreline
Some other past approached,
Mine perhaps, so lost to memory
That it seemed a stranger,

Or maybe it was the lost childhood
Of the sea itself,
Wandering the desolate evening
While the clouds grew faint

And the tides turned their longing inward.
It was a pattern equally rich
In nostalgia and redemption,
A shimmering uncatchable scene

More often glimpsed through the
Fogged channels of death
Or a dream's tiny doorway
Then in the quiet, oceanic depths

Of some imperfect poem
Lying on its back at the notebook's margin;
Poor, beached mammal of music,
Unidentifiable headstone of song.

Images

I found a father who sings
In the changeless light.
I found a son with two torn-out heart strings.

In the old wind a young bird
Is taking shape
With twin eggs burning in his throat.

On the way to an unspecified kingdom
A pilgrim falls down
And weeps.

Utterly amazed, a fish is staring
Through the stream's blue pupils
Wondering if he is king.

In my body's half-spent pastures
A demon and an angel
Have begun to wrestle.

I believe death arrived long ago
On a star crashing through the
Dreaming ether.

He crept into the garden
And slid one long hand
Down the woman's thigh.

Since then we have lived secretly burning
To touch our own frail hands
Against the moon's crescent,

Have lived with one arm building wings
Across endless abysses,
With one arm touching

The dark, hermetic seeds.

Creatures

The wind breaking
On the rutted road
Is like the voice
Of some other world
Calling through the early
Dark of spring.
And I lift my hand,
Which is your hand,
To thank the generous elements
Who have opened this tiny door
Between that blossoming other kingdom
And our own ruinous kind of being.

From the Window at 2 AM

Isolation. And the strange drip of rain.
Candescent heart in the unlit body.
The brain, a thorough demon.

We come from one place
And end in another.
In between, a sloughing wind.

From a pill, cosmic understanding.
From a pen, small strokes
Of song.

Outside, a car jettisons across
The darkness, backfires,
Loses the road.

At the same time, an owl haunts the tree line.
Two calls, equally wild
In the malfeasance of night.

And somewhere, my own scream
Looking, love-struck, for my mouth.

Force

Nothing more holy than the snow
Outside the window
And the thunder inside
Burning all night.

Nothing besides the earthenware
Glaze of stars
On the roof of forests
While the sun goes down.

Nothing besides the deep, heart-bound thirst,
The internal plant-like longing
That burgeons from the mouth
And flowers overhead.

That subterranean machine
That compels the body,
That rages wars,
That sings of God.

Nothing more holy besides
The magnetic, unnamable force
That welds our lives
Firmly to the earth.

In The House Magisterial

The immense and stumbling wind
Passes through a field
Into a house where a portrait
Of Christ slides from the wall
Onto the azure floorboards.
Overhead, the loneliness of childhood
Wanders the second floor
And dances in the strange, abandoned darkness.
Love, which is as real and full of light
As an apricot on winter evenings,
Sees itself shining in a mirror
Overrun by dust.
Of what remains from the old, long-gone inhabitants
I find only withered, flaking furniture
And a dirty, jewel-encrusted star.

Alembic

There is an alembic,
Burgundy, deep-light, surface-dark,
That I drink when my heart
Is most at stake.

It alternately transfigures
Or degrades the life around me.
It is a gamble.
A tincture full of concentrated chance.

At the onset my love may become
An angel, or in a twist
A whole crowd of ghosts
That I sneak and dart from.

It may carry me, bone-drunk,
Through the stars,
Or lay me down in a swarming
Mat of insects and decay.

Whatever happens, I take it happily.
Scared of the middle outcome,
The sober, latched-up center,
The option that doesn't sing.

Signals for Belief

The simplest, most incommunicable truth
Is a small stone at the bottom of the heart,
An intimation among the bile,
Among the patchwork of perjury and blood.
It doesn't sing like love,
Or burn in the bowels like hate or anger.
It barely simmers even when the most glaring space
Opens for its presence.
Instead it is like a hint of the unknown
That comes and goes with the wind's discretion.
An instinct that shudders in the carpentry
Of bone.
A subtle premonition
In a backed-up voice box.
It's a slow, lugubrious butterfly
That occasionally starts up
From the intestinal thatch-roof,
Lifts its one-of-a-kind body
Up through the diaphragm
And disappears through the pear-shaped
Clouds of morning.

Wild Pears

Describing the dawn
As precisely as equating equations
Is a task that language cannot do.
We must substitute the perfection of the moment
For the lesser perfection of words,
Though they may be the most perfect thing
We have.
And it is its own kind of beauty
To inaccurately describe the morning sky
As a forest erupting into flames
While the clouds burst from the rubble
Like wild pears.

Lantern

We are full of hidden fires.
The autumn of the body
Is the birth
Of another light,
Another self,
Hinged to this one.
When the wick is snubbed
The other lantern is roused
From dust.
We have been carrying it, all along,
Year after year:
Cold candle,
Patient fuel,
Loss, the sure ignition.
And what we thought
Was the end
Of a dwindling circuit
Proves just a catalyst.
A spark floating
On through darkness.

Trees from Eight Angles

Invariably, these statues sing.
Wrought-up in the darkened landscape
By the combing wind

They sway in their emerald music
While overhead, the small muscles
Of the stars work the universe.

They are the old, gnarled fingers
From the earth's deep clutches.
The towering alphabet from which the birds

Offer tiny lessons.
They carry little scraps of darkness
On their breezy shoulders

And drop them over us on summer days.
They eat the dead and resurrect
Their mottled bodies,

Offer fruit in the starving sun.
They give form to our endless families,
Dust upon inherited dust.

And when a great love has entered
Through our lives,
We lay our shared breath beneath them

While they drop, one by one,
Their perfect heart-shaped cherries
Into our dreaming mouths.

Old Honey

Full of longing and delicately stored
In the small earthenware jar of honey
The dragonfly has waited forty years
To steal from its chrysalis
And be spread.

Meditation on a Sunporch in Maine

We disappear, and are bound to our passage
Like hoists in the bulwark of death.
With no eternity to speak of
There are only fruits carefully arranged
On a plate in summer.
There is only the gestures of trees
In ambient light as the sun goes down.
When I think of the body
Under the shelter of dirt in a New England cemetery
I think not of resurrection
But the exquisite delicacy of each day.
The porcelain of time that cracks
And reforms in unexpected jolts.
The near unbearable perfection
Of sitting next to you on a sunporch in Maine
After a summer of traveling, and the mantra
Spoken softly and intently in the heart:
This too will pass, this too will pass.

Seth Jani grew up in the western mountains of Maine, in a town seemingly outside the reaches of time. He spent his formative years exploring the forests and lakes, befriending wild animals, and learning the truth of things from the rocks and trees.

Since then he has lived all over the country, building houses in New Orleans, constructing trails in Vermont, and planting native plants in the Mojave Desert and the mountains of the Pacific Northwest.

He currently resides in Seattle, WA, where he is editor-in-chief of Seven CirclePress (www.sevencirclepress.com), an independent publisher of poetry and short fiction.

His own work has been published widely in such places as *The American Poetry Journal*, *Chiron Review*, *Pretty Owl Poetry*, *Abyss & Apex*, *Phantom Drift*, *The Hamilton Stone Review*, *Common Ground Review*, *Gingerbread House*, *Gravel* and *Zetetic: A Record of Unusual Inquiry*.

More about him and his work can be found at www.sethjani.com.